T0070985

John Rutter

Anthems and Choral Songs

for upper-voice choirs

(sopranos and altos, and/or boys' unchanged voices)

MUSIC DEPARTMENT

OXFORD
UNIVERSITY PRESS

OXFORD
UNIVERSITY PRESS

Great Clarendon Street, Oxford OX2 6DP,
United Kingdom

Oxford University Press is a department of the University of Oxford.
It furthers the University's objective of excellence in research, scholarship,
and education by publishing worldwide. Oxford is a registered trade mark of
Oxford University Press in the UK and in certain other countries

This collection © Oxford University Press 2019

John Rutter has asserted his right under the Copyright, Designs
and Patents Act, 1988, to be identified as the Composer of these Works

First published 2019

Impression: 1

All rights reserved. No part of this publication may be reproduced,
stored in a retrieval system, or transmitted, in any form or by any means,
without the prior permission in writing of Oxford University Press

Permission to perform the works in this anthology in public
(except in the course of divine worship) should normally be obtained from
a local performing right licensing organization, unless the owner or the occupier
of the premises being used already holds a licence from such an organization.
Likewise, permission to make and exploit a recording of these works
should be obtained from a local mechanical copyright licensing organization

Enquiries concerning reproduction outside the scope of the above
should be directed to the Music Rights Department, Oxford University Press, at
music.permissions.uk@oup.com or at the address above

ISBN 978-0-19-353023-2

Music originated on Sibelius
Printed in Great Britain on acid-free paper by
Halstan & Co. Ltd, Amersham, Bucks.

Contents

A Clare Benediction	5
A flower remembered	12
A Gaelic Blessing	19
All things bright and beautiful	24
For the beauty of the earth	29
God be in my head	38
Look at the world	41
The Lord bless you and keep you	51
The Music's Always There With You	56

for Clare College, Cambridge

A Clare Benediction

Words and music by
JOHN RUTTER

© Oxford University Press 1998 and 2019. Photocopying this copyright material is ILLEGAL.

16
SOPRANOS 1 and 2
mp
you; may his spi - rit be ev-er by your side. When you
21
cresc.
sleep, may his an - gels watch o - ver you; when you
cresc.
25
mf
SOPRANOS and ALTOS
mf cresc.
wake, may he fill you with his grace: May you
mf
29
S.
f ma dolce
dim.
mp
love him and serve him all your days, Then in
A.
f ma dolce
dim.
love him and serve him all your days,
dim.

33
(SOPRANOS 1 and 2)
hea - ven may you see his face.
mp
con Ped.
38
SOPRANO 1
mf
2. May the Lord's lov-ing kind - ness sur-
SOPRANO 2
mf
2. May the Lord's lov-ing kind - ness sur-
ALTO
mf
2. May the Lord's lov-ing kind - ness sur-
poco cresc.
mf
43
-round you; keep you safe as you jour-ney on your
-round you; keep you safe as you jour-ney on your
-round you; keep you safe as you jour-ney on your

47
way: May he lead you and in-
way: May he lead you and in-
way: May he lead you
51
-spire you as he grants you the gift of each new
- spire you as he grants you the gift of each new
and in - spire you as he grants you the gift of each new

55
p
day.
Ah
(mf)
day.
May he bless all your loved ones and
p
day.
Ah
mp
59
mf
Ev-'ry friend, ev-'ry stran-ger at your
che-rish them;
Ev-'ry friend, ev-'ry stran-ger at your
mf
ev-'ry stran-ger at your
cresc.
mf

63
cresc.
f
door: In the name of his Son, our
door: In the name of his Son, his Son, our
door: In the name of his Son, his Son, our
67
poco rall.
dim.
a tempo
p
Sa - viour Christ, May God bless you, now and ev -
Sa - viour Christ, May God bless you, now and ev -
Sa - viour Christ,

72
mp
p
- er - more, may God bless you now and
mp
- er - more, may God bless you
p
mp
may God bless you
mp
p
77
rall.
poco meno mosso
rit.
dim.
pp
ev - - er - more, now and ev - er - more.
p
dim.
pp
now and ev - er - more, now and ev - er - more.
p
dim.
pp
now and ev - er - more, now and ev - er - more.
rall.
poco meno mosso
rit.
p
dim.
pp

in memory of the victims of the Tohoku area earthquake and tsunami, March 2011

A flower remembered

Words and music by
JOHN RUTTER

Slow and reflective ♩ = 60

PIANO

p *pp* *mp* *cantabile*

unhurried, poco rubato

Ped. *Ped.*

4

SOPRANOS (with Altos ad lib.)

p thoughtful and unhurried

1. A flow'r re-mem-bered can nev-er

legato sim. *p*

Ped. sim.

8

wi-ther: For ev-er bloom-ing as bright as day, Its fra-grance

Also published in its original version for mixed voices (978-0-19-340482-3)

© Collegium Music Publications 2014 and 2019. Exclusively licensed worldwide to Oxford University Press.
Photocopying this copyright material is ILLEGAL.

11
mp
lin-g'ring like mu-sic soft-ly play-ing, A gen-tle voice that's say-ing, 'I'll nev-er fade a-
mp
14
SOPRANO 1
p
A
-way.' I hear the e - choes of ma-ny voi-ces; Some-times they're
SOPRANO 2
p
-way.' I hear the e - choes of ma-ny voi-ces; Some-times they're
ALTO
p
I hear the e - choes of ma-ny voi-ces; Some-times they're
A
p
17
mp
mf
di - stant, some-times so clear; Through all the sounds of life they seem to
mp
mf
di - stant, some-times so clear; Through all the sounds of life they seem to
mp
mf
di - stant, some-times so clear; Through all the sounds of life they seem to
mp
mf

20
p
poco rit.
a tempo
pp
whis-per, 'Will you re-mem-ber, will you re-mem-ber?'
whis-per, 'Will you re-mem-ber, will you re-mem-ber?'
whis-per, 'Will you re-mem-ber, will you re-mem-ber?'
poco rit.
a tempo
24
SOLO VOICE
or SEMI-CHORUS
mf dolce
2. The birds fly
mf
mp

*or other vocalized sound, like 'Ah' or 'Oo'

32
melt - ed, But still I see their beau - ty, these scenes of long a -
mm mm
mm mm
mm mm
34
(col tutti)
- go.
p mp cresc.
The birds still fly in o-ther val-leys; The snows have
p mp cresc.
The birds still fly in o-ther val-leys; The snows have
p mp cresc.
The birds still fly in o-ther val-leys; The snows have
mp cresc.

Largamente
37
turned to flow - ing streams; All things must
turned to flow - ing streams; All things must
turned to flow - ing streams; All things must
Largamente
39
C
pass, but me - mo - ries are last - ing:
pass, but me - mo - ries are last - ing:
pass, but me - mo - ries are last - ing: We will re -
C

41
mp
p
We will re - mem-ber, we will re - mem - ber,
mp
p
We will re - mem-ber, we will re - mem - ber,
p
-mem-ber, we will re - mem - ber, we will re -
mp
p
molto rit. al fine
44
pp
we will re - mem - ber.
pp
we will re - mem - ber.
pp
-mem - ber, we will re - mem - ber.
molto rit. al fine
pp
Ped.

A Gaelic Blessing

Words by William Sharp (1855–1905)
adapted by JR

JOHN RUTTER

© 1978, 2016, and 2019 The Royal School of Church Music. All rights reserved. Photocopying this copyright material is ILLEGAL.

9
air to you, Deep peace of the qui-et
air to you, Deep peace of the
air to you, Deep peace of the
13
mp
earth to you, Deep peace of the shin-ing
mp
earth to you, Deep, deep peace of the
mp
earth to you, Deep, deep peace of the
mp

*If preferred, these four bars may be sung an octave higher.

25
p
light on you, Deep peace of
light on you, Deep peace of
Deep peace of
29
cresc.
mf
Christ, of Christ the
Christ, of Christ the
Christ, of Christ the

33
f
dim.
light of the world to you,
f
dim.
light of the world to you,
f
dim.
light of the world to you,
f
dim.

37
mp
dim.
rall.
pp
Deep peace of Christ to you.
mp
dim.
pp
Deep peace of Christ to you.
mp
dim.
pp
Deep peace of Christ to you.
rall.
mp
dim.
pp

Commissioned by Westminster Choir College for Helen Kemp

All things bright and beautiful

Words by Mrs C. F. Alexander (1823–95)

JOHN RUTTER

© Oxford University Press 1983 and 2019. Photocopying this copyright material is ILLEGAL.

17
mf
Each lit-tle bird that sings, He made their glow-ing co-lours, He
mf
21
SOPRANOS and ALTOS
mf
made their ti-ny wings. All things bright and beau-ti-ful, All
(mf)
25
cresc.
f dolce
crea-tures great and small, All things wise and won-der-ful, The
cresc.
29
SOPRANOS
mf
Lord God made them all. The
f dolce
mf

B
33
pur - ple-head - ed moun - tain, The riv - er run - ning by, The
Ped.
Ped.
Ped.
37
sun - set, and the morn - ing That bright - ens up the sky;
40
ALTOS
mp
The cold wind in the win - ter, The plea - sant sum - mer sun,
mp
Ped.
Ped.
sim.
44
S.
SOPRANOS
mp
cresc.
mf
The ripe fruits in the gar - den, He made them ev - 'ry
cresc.
mf

poco rit.
a tempo
C
SOPRANOS and ALTOS
48
mf
one:
All things bright and beau-ti-ful, All crea-tures great and
(mf)
52
small,
All things wise and won-der-ful, The Lord God made them all.
56
cresc.
He gave us eyes to see them, And
cresc.
59
f
lips that we might tell How great is God Al -
f

62
unis.
- might - y, Who has made all things well.
65
D
(f)
All things bright and beau-ti - ful, All crea - tures great and
(f)
Ped.
sim.
68
small, All things wise and won - der-ful,
mf dim.
l.h.
72
rall.
mp
dim.
a tempo
p
The Lord God made them all.
mp
dim.
p
Ped.
76
rall.
pp
Ped.
Ped.

Commissioned by the Texas Choral Directors' Association

For the beauty of the earth

Words by F. S. Pierpoint (1835–1917)

JOHN RUTTER

© Oxford University Press 1980 and 2019. Photocopying this copyright material is ILLEGAL.

17
love which from our birth O-ver and a-
21
-round us lies, o-ver and a-round us lies: Lord of
25
mf
all, to thee we raise
mf
29
mp
This our joy - ful hymn of praise.
mp

A
33
SOPRANO mf
ALTO
2. For the beau - ty of each
mf
37
hour
Of the day and of the
41
S.
night,
Hill and vale,
and tree and
A.
night,
Hill and vale,
45
flower,
Sun and moon and stars of light:
and tree and flower,
Sun and moon and

49
f
Lord of all, to thee we
f
3
stars of light: Lord of all, to thee we
3
cresc.
f
53
mf
raise This our joy - ful hymn of
mf
raise This our hymn of
mf
57
praise.
praise.
mp espress.
Ped. Ped.

61
B
p
3. For the joy of
mp espress.
3. For the joy of hu - man love,
B
p dolce
65
love,
Bro - ther, sis - ter, pa - rent,
Bro - ther, sis - ter, pa - rent, child,
Friends on
69
child, Friends on earth,
and friends a - bove,
earth,
and friends a - bove,
For all gen - tle

73
(p)
For all gen - tle thoughts and mild:
thoughts and mild,
for all gen-tle thoughts and mild:
Lord of
77
mf
Lord of all,
to thee we raise
mf
all to thee we raise
mf
81
p
Our joy-ful hymn of praise.
mp
This our joy - ful hymn of praise.
mp
cresc.

85
C
f
4. For each per - fect gift of thine
f
4. For each per - fect gift of thine
C
f
89
To our race so free - ly giv - en,
To our race so free - ly giv - en,
mf
Gra - ces
mf
93
mf
Gra - ces hu-man and di - vine,
hu - - man and di - vine,
Flow'rs of earth and

97
cresc.
Ah
Ah
cresc.
buds of heav'n,
flow'rs of earth and buds of heav'n:
cresc.
100
f
Lord of all, to thee we
f
Lord of all, to thee we
3
f
103
D (♪ = ♪)
mf
raise
This our joy - ful
mf
raise
This
D (♪ = ♪)
mf

107
hymn of praise,
our joy - ful hymn of praise,
rall.
(rallentando al fine)
111
p
This our joy - ful hymn of
p
our hymn of
rall.
(rallentando al fine)
dim.
p
114
molto rall.
praise.
praise.
molto rall.
(p)

God be in my head

Words from the Sarum Primer (1514)

JOHN RUTTER

© Oxford University Press 1970 and 2019. Assigned by Oxford University Press Inc. 2010.
Photocopying this copyright material is ILLEGAL.

9
p
look - - - ing. God be in my mouth
p
look - - - ing. God be in my mouth
p
look - - - ing. God be in my mouth
p
13
mf
p
and in my speak - - - ing. God be
mf
p
and in my speak - - - - ing. God be
mf
p
and in my speak - - - - ing. God be
mf
p

17
Poco meno mosso
pp
in mine heart and in my think - ing. God be
in mine heart and in my think - ing. God be
in mine heart and in my think - ing. God be
Poco meno mosso
pp
21
rit.
pp
ppp
at my end and in my de - part - - ing.
at my end and in my de - part - - ing.
at my end and in my de - part - - ing.
rit.
pp
ppp

in celebration of the 70th anniversary of the Council for the Protection of Rural England

Look at the world

Words and music by
JOHN RUTTER

© Oxford University Press 1996 and 2019. Photocopying this copyright material is ILLEGAL.

17
ALTOS
mf
Look at the world: so ma-ny joys and won - ders,
Look at the hills, look at the trees and moun-tains,
21
So ma-ny mi - ra - cles a - long our way.
Val-ley and flow - ing ri - ver, field and plain:
A
25
SOPRANO 1
mf
S.1
Praise to thee, O Lord, for all cre - a - tion,
SOPRANO 2
mf
S.2
Praise to thee, O Lord, for all cre - a - tion,
ALTO
mf
A.
Praise to thee, O Lord, for all cre - a - tion,
A
mf

29
S.1
Give us thank - ful hearts, that we may see:
S.2
Give us thank - ful hearts, that we may see:
A.
Give us thank - ful hearts, that we may see:
33
dim.
All the gifts we share, and ev - 'ry bless - ing,
dim.
All the gifts we share, and ev - 'ry bless - ing,
dim.
All the gifts we share, and ev - 'ry bless - ing,
dim.

37
mp
S.1
S.2
1.
All things come of thee.
mp
A.
All things come of thee.
1.
mp
cresc.
41
Back to p. 41
2.
thee.
thee.
thee.
mf
2.
mf
45
B
ALTOS
mp legato
3. Think of the spring,
mp legato

49
think of the warmth of sum-mer Bring-ing the har-vest be -
53
-fore the win - ter's cold.
SOPRANOS
mp legato
Ev -'ry-thing
56
grows, ev -'ry-thing has a sea - son,
59
Till it is ga-thered to the Fa - ther's fold:

*Small notes are for rehearsal only.

73
ev - 'ry bless - ing, All things come of thee.
ev - 'ry bless - ing, All things come of thee.
ev - 'ry bless - ing, All things come of thee.
p
p cresc.
78
D
SOPRANOS and ALTOS
f
4. Ev-'ry good
(cresc.)
f
82
gift, all that we need and che - rish

85
unis.
Comes from the Lord in to - ken of his
88
ALTOS
mf
love;
We are his hands,
mf
91
SOPRANOS and ALTOS
mf
stew-ards of all his boun - ty;
His is the
94
cresc.
earth, and his the heav'ns a - bove:
cresc.

97
E
f
Praise to thee, O Lord, for all cre - a - tion,
Praise to thee, O Lord, for all cre - a - tion,
Praise to thee, O Lord, for all cre - a - tion,
101
dim.
Give us thank - ful hearts, that we may see:
Give us thank - ful hearts, that we may see:
Give us thank - ful hearts, that we may see:
105
mf
All the gifts we share, and ev - 'ry bless - ing,
All the gifts we share, and ev - 'ry bless - ing,
All the gifts we share, and ev - 'ry bless - ing,

109
mp
All things come of thee,
mp
All things come of thee,
mp
All things come of thee,
mp
dim.
rall. al fine
113
p
all things come of thee.
p
all things come of thee.
p
all things come of thee.
rall. al fine
p

The Lord bless you and keep you

Numbers 6: 24

JOHN RUTTER

© Oxford University Press 1981 and 2019. Photocopying this copyright material is ILLEGAL.

10
1st SOPRANOS
S.1
you. The Lord bless you and keep you: The
2nd SOPRANOS
S.2
you. The Lord bless you and keep you: The
ALTOS
A.
p dolce e legato
The Lord bless you and keep you: The
13
mp
Lord make his face to shine up-on you, to shine up-on you and be
mp
Lord make his face to shine up-on you, to shine up-on you, to
mp
Lord make his face to shine up-on you, to shine up-on you, to
mp

16
S.1
gra - cious, and be gra - cious un-to you: The
S.2
shine up-on you and be gra - cious un-to you: The
A.
shine up-on you and be gra - cious un-to you:
19
cresc.
mf
S.1
S.2
Lord lift up the light of his coun - te-nance up -
cresc.
mf
22
mp cresc.
mf
S.1
S.2
- on you, the Lord lift up the light of his coun - te-nance up -
mp cresc.
mf
A.
the Lord lift up the light of his coun - te-nance up -
mp cresc.
mf

26
(unis.)
mp
dim.
S.1
S.2
-on you and give you peace,
A.
-on you
mp
p
and give you
dim.
mp
dim.
p
30
pp
p
and give you peace, and give you
dim.
pp
p
peace, and give you peace, and give you
dim.
pp
cresc.
p
34
poco rit.
a tempo
mp
mf
S.1
peace. A - - - men, a - -
S.2
mf
peace. a - -
A.
peace.
poco rit.
a tempo
mp
cresc.
mf

38
f
mf
- men, a - - - men, a - men, a -
- men, a - men, a - men, a -
a - men, a - - men, a -
a - men, a - - men, a -
cresc.
dim.
42
mp
rall.
molto rall.
p dim.
pp
- - men, a - men, a - - - men.
-men, a - - - - men, a - - - men.
-men, a - - men, a - - - men.
- - men, a - - men, a - men, a - men.
dim.

for Per-Anders Sjöberg and friends

The Music's Always There With You

Words and music by
JOHN RUTTER

© Oxford University Press 1989 and 2019. Assigned by Hinshaw Music Inc. 2016. Photocopying this copyright material is ILLEGAL.

18
-rade, And youth be-come a time you just re-
21
A
-call; But the good times to - geth - er seem so
25
mf
ma - gi-cal: Like mu - sic that lasts your whole life
mf
ma - gi-cal: Like mu - sic that lasts your whole life
mf

29
through;
mp
Ah
through;
mp
When it's end-ed it nev - er real - ly
dim.
mp
33
unis. p
'Cos the mu - sic's al - ways there with
dies a - way
p
'Cos the mu - sic's al - ways there with
p
37
you.
B
mf
Ev-'ry
you.
mf
Ev-'ry
cresc.
B
mf

41
new day could be a time of har - mo-ny If
new day could be a time of har - mo-ny If
45
mp
peo - ple could on - ly be in tune: All the
mp
peo - ple could on - ly be in tune: All the
dim.
49
(unis.)
vi - sions you could share, ma-gic cas - tles in the air Seem to
vi - sions you could share, ma-gic cas - tles in the air Seem to
mp delicato

53
fade a - way and van - ish all too soon;
But the
fade a - way and van - ish all too soon;
But the
cresc.
57
C (unis.)
mf
ma - gic you share when you make mu - sic
Won't
mf
ma - gic you share when you make mu - sic
Won't
C
mf
61
mp
leave you when the time has come to part;
And it
mp
leave you when the time has come to part;
And it
dim.

65
feels like you nev - er have to say good - bye, 'Cos the
feels like you nev - er have to say good - bye, 'Cos the
mp
69
mu - sic's al - ways there in your heart.
f warmly
But the
mu - sic's al - ways there in your heart.
f warmly
But the
cresc.
Ped.
73
D
ma - gic you share when you make mu - sic Won't
ma - gic you share when you make mu - sic Won't
ma - gic you share when you make mu - sic Won't
ma - gic you share when you make mu - sic Won't
D
f warmly
Ped.
sim.

77
mp
leave you when the time has come to part: And it
mp
leave you when the time has come to part: And it
leave you when the time has come to part:
leave you when the time has come to part:
3
dim.
81
Freely
rall.
feels like you nev - er have to say good - bye,
feels like you nev - er have to say good - bye,
mp
Oo 'Cos the
mp
Oo 'Cos the
Freely
rall.
mp

85
a tempo
mf
'Cos the mu - sic's al - ways there, the
mf
'Cos the mu - sic's al - ways there, the
cresc.
mf
mu - sic's al - ways there, 'Cos the mu - sic's al - ways there, the
cresc.
mf
mu - sic's al - ways there, 'Cos the mu - sic's al - ways there, the
a tempo
cresc.
mf
89
poco rall. al fine
dim.
p
mu - sic's al - ways there in your heart.
dim.
p
mu - sic's al - ways there in your heart.
dim.
p
mu - sic's al - ways there in your heart.
dim.
p
mu - sic's al - ways there in your heart.
poco rall. al fine
mp
p
Ped.